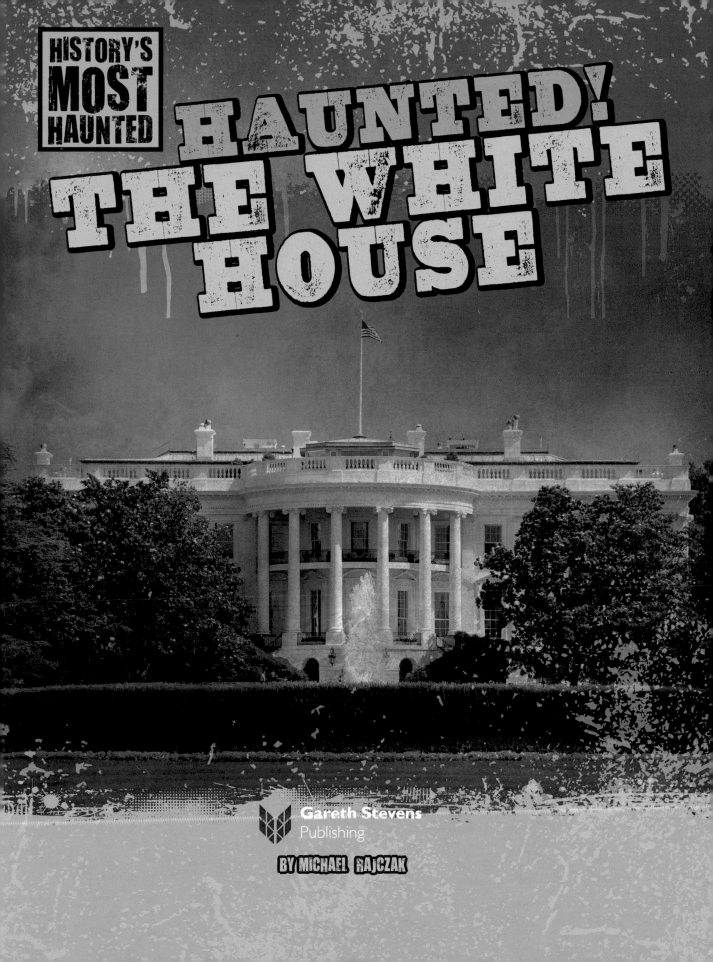

HISTORY'S MOST HAUNTED

HAUNTED! THE WHITE HOUSE

Gareth Stevens
Publishing

BY MICHAEL RAJCZAK

Please visit our website, www.garethstevens.com. For a free color catalog of all our high-quality books, call toll free 1-800-542-2595 or fax 1-877-542-2596.

Library of Congress Cataloging-in-Publication Data

Rajczak, Michael.
Haunted! White House / by Michael Rajczak.
  p. cm. —(History's most haunted)
Includes index.
ISBN 978-1-4339-9269-8 (pbk.)
ISBN 978-1-4339-9270-4 (6-pack)
ISBN 978-1-4339-9268-1 (library binding)
1. White House (Washington, D.C.)—Juvenile literature. 2. Washington (D.C.)—Buildings, structures, etc.—Juvenile literature. 3. Ghosts—Washington (D.C.)—Juvenile literature. 4. Haunted houses—Washington (D.C.)—Juvenile literature. 5. Haunted places—Juvenile literature. I. Rajczak, Michael. II. Title.
BF1472.U6 R35 2014
133.1—dc23

First Edition

Published in 2014 by
Gareth Stevens Publishing
111 East 14th Street, Suite 349
New York, NY 10003

Copyright © 2014 Gareth Stevens Publishing

Designer: Nicholas Domiano
Editor: Kristen Rajczak

Photo credits: Cover, p. 1 Vacclav/Shutterstock.com; p. 5 John Plumbe/Wikimedia Commons; p. 6 Time Life Pictures/Time & Life Pictures/Getty Images; p. 7 Dmitri Kessel/TIME & LIFE Images/Getty Images; p. 8 John Vanderlyn/Wikimedia Commons; p. 9 George Munger/ Wikimedia Commons; p 10 White House Photostream/Wikimedia Commons; p. 11 Gilbert Stuart/Wikimedia Commons; p. 12 Ralph Eleaser Whiteside Earl/Wikimedia Commons; p. 13 Magnus Manske/Wikimedia Commons; p. 14 iStockphoto/Thinkstock.com; p. 15 AR Pictures/Shutterstock.com; p. 16 Currier & Ives/Wikimedia Commons; p. 17 Hulton Archive/Getty Images; p. 19 Bill O'Leary/The Washington Post/Getty Images; p. 21 Songquan Deng/Shutterstock.com; p. 23 Levin Corbin Handy/Wikimedia Commons; p. 24 White House Photo Office/Wikimedia Commons; p. 25 Alexcoldcasefan/Wikimedia Commons; p. 27 Stephen St. John/ National Geographic/Getty Images; p. 29 Joel Sartore/National Geographic/Getty Images.

Printed in the United States of America

CPSIA compliance information: Batch #CS13GS: For further information contact Gareth Stevens, New York, New York at 1-800-542-2595.

CONTENTS

Words in the glossary appear in **bold** type the first time they are used in the text.

THE OBSTINATE MR. BURNS

The first president might be responsible for the first White House ghost! When George Washington and city designer Pierre L'Enfant were planning the construction of Washington, DC, a miserable man named David Burns owned the land where they wanted to build the presidential **mansion**. President Washington called him the "**obstinate** Mr. Burns."

While selling the land made Burns wealthy, he really hadn't wanted to do it. This may be the reason why his ghost has been reported in the White House! White House staffers have heard a voice claiming "I am Mr. Burns" from above the Oval Office.

MANY GHOSTS

David Burns is just one ghost that's said to occupy the big, white house at 1600 Pennsylvania Avenue in Washington, DC. The spirits that remain have become stories told to visitors as well as the White House staff. Even presidents have claimed to witness hauntings!

David Burns's ill temper remained until his death, as did his dislike at being bullied out of part of his property.

ABIGAIL ADAMS

Abigail Adams was the wife of the second president, John Adams. They were the first occupants of the White House. At that time, it was common for the First Lady to help in the house's upkeep: preparing meals, performing basic cleaning, and doing **laundry**.

ABIGAIL ADAMS

Abigail's ghost was first seen during the administration of President Howard Taft. In fact, President Taft himself reported seeing her ghost float through closed doors on the second floor! Abigail's ghost has been seen in the East Room walking with her arms out as if carrying a basket of clean clothes. Her appearances have been accompanied by the smells of soap and damp laundry.

The ghost of the second First Lady may still haunt the East Room.

NOT TOO GRAND FOR LAUNDRY!

When President and Mrs. Adams first came to the White House, parts of it were still under construction. Since many rooms were drafty or damp, Abigail Adams used the grand East Room on the first floor to hang her laundry. It was the warmest, driest place in the house!

THE BRITISH SOLDIER

During the **War of 1812**, President James Madison and his wife, Dolley, had to flee the White House. British soldiers were on their way. A large dinner had been prepared, so the soldiers helped themselves to the meal. Afterward, they took many valuables and set the White House on fire, burning it to the ground.

Since that night, the ghost of a British soldier holding a flaming torch has been reported on the White House grounds. More disturbing, another soldier's ghost has been seen by overnight guests staying in one of the upstairs bedrooms. The ghostly soldier tried to set their bed on fire!

PRESIDENT MADISON

The flames from the burning of the White House lit up the sky on August 24, 1814. This painting shows what it looked like after the fire.

FIRE AND RETALIATION

The British burned the White House and other government buildings, including the unfinished Capitol. They did so in **retaliation** for the American burning of villages along the Great Lakes in British-controlled Canada. The British only held Washington, DC, briefly. President Madison and Dolley were able to return to the city in just a few days.

DOLLEY MADISON

Dolley Madison was the nation's third First Lady to live in the White House. She created the original White House Rose Garden. About 100 years later, President Woodrow Wilson's wife, Edith, decided to remove the Rose Garden. Workers who were about to start the job reported that the ghost of Dolley Madison appeared and seemed angry that her garden was being removed. The workers refused to destroy the garden, and Mrs. Wilson abandoned the idea.

Dolley Madison's ghost is still occasionally seen walking through the garden. The sudden smell of roses in the White House is credited to Dolley Madison's ghost, too.

Dolley Madison was considered a popular hostess known for planning lavish dinner parties. Is her ghost as good a hostess?

MORE THAN ONE HAUNTING

While the White House was repaired, the Madisons made their home up the street at the Octagon House. Today, visitors sometimes report the strong smell of lilacs there and associate it with the ghost of Dolley Madison. She's said to have worn lilac-scented perfume during her life.

ANDREW JACKSON

In life, Andrew Jackson was a strong military leader devoted to his country. However, he was known to be disagreeable and have a quick temper, too!

During the **American Civil War**, Mary Todd Lincoln first encountered Jackson's ghost swearing and stomping about in his old bedroom, the Rose Room. Near the end of **World War II**, President Harry Truman mentioned Jackson's spirit as one he felt around him when he wrote about the spooky sounds of the White House. In the 1950s, Jackson's ghost was seen again. Jackson's ghost also has been reported at his old mansion, the Hermitage, in Tennessee!

ANDREW JACKSON

Loud laughter or cursing heard in the Rose Room might be Andrew Jackson's ghost!

THE BELL WITCH

In 1819, Jackson heard the tale of a witch plaguing the farm of a local family. He and some friends went out one evening to challenge the witch. Jackson and friends were slapped, pinched, and kicked throughout the night. Jackson later said he would rather fight the British than the Bell Witch!

A GHOST IN THE ATTIC

William Henry Harrison had been president for only a month when he died from an illness called pneumonia. Not long after, workers and White House staff began to hear strange sounds in the third-floor attic.

Upon investigation, several people encountered the ghost of President Harrison! He seemed to be looking for something in the storage area. Harrison's ghost appears to have bluish skin and is often seen and heard coughing. Some say he is looking for medicine to cure his illness, while others think he is looking for his **inaugural** speech.

WILLIAM HENRY HARRISON

Harrison died of pneumonia— but perhaps a curse has caused his spirit to remain in the White House!

DEATH BY CURSE?

After the shocking death of Harrison after just a month in office, rumors began that a curse was placed upon him and future presidents because of wrongs done to Native Americans. Beginning with Harrison, seven presidents whose election years ended with a zero died while in office. An eighth, Ronald Reagan, **survived** an **assassin's** bullet.

15

ABRAHAM LINCOLN

The ghost of Abraham Lincoln has been encountered more than any other in the White House. His wife is said to have felt his presence in the days after his assassination. First Lady Grace Coolidge was the first person to report seeing Lincoln's ghost looking thoughtfully out the window toward the Potomac River. Even Eleanor Roosevelt said she often sensed Lincoln's presence!

During World War II, there were several instances of people witnessing Lincoln's ghost. One White House staff member was so startled that he ran screaming out a door. Another entered the Lincoln Bedroom and saw the ghost of President Lincoln pulling on his boots.

Abraham Lincoln was assassinated by John Wilkes Booth while he was at Ford's Theater in Washington, DC.

DREAMING OF DEATH

Shortly before he was killed, Abraham Lincoln dreamed he was walking through the White House. He heard people crying. When Lincoln entered the East Room, he saw a person wrapped in funeral clothing with soldiers standing guard. Lincoln asked: "Who is dead in the White House?" A soldier answered: "The president. He was killed by an assassin."

17

Many people who have stayed in the Lincoln Bedroom at the White House have heard ghostly footsteps outside in the hallway. Others have heard knocks at the door. During a visit in 1942, Queen Wilhelmina of the Netherlands answered a knocking at the door and said she came face-to-face with Abraham Lincoln's ghost.

Another time, British Prime Minister Winston Churchill was returning in a towel from taking a bath. He opened the door and saw Lincoln warming himself by the fireplace. Churchill is reported to have said, "Good evening, Mr. President. You seem to have me at a disadvantage." Lincoln looked at him, smiled, and then disappeared.

OFFICE GHOST

Abraham Lincoln didn't use the Lincoln Bedroom as his sleep chamber. He used the room as his presidential office. The suite of two rooms, the second of which is a bathroom, was used for meetings until the West Wing was added in the early 1900s. Then, the room became a bedroom.

Staying the night in the Lincoln Bedroom could be a pretty eerie experience if you find yourself in the company of a ghost!

THE DEMON CAT

The basement of the White House is another spooky area. Over the years, there have been reports of a mysterious black cat prowling down there. It appears at first as a kitten but changes into a scary, tiger-sized beast with glowing eyes! The cat tends to make its appearance as if to warn of a national tragedy.

The cat had been seen before the stock market crash of the late 1920s, before the assassination of President John F. Kennedy, and, some say, before the **terrorist** attacks on September 11, 2001. As early as 1862, and again in 1898, White House guards claim to have shot at the menacing creature near a basement storage area.

HAUNTING ALL OVER DC

The White House isn't the only place in Washington, DC, that is haunted by a demon cat. A similar beast is said to inhabit the basement area of the US Capitol. A Capitol guard reported that something lunged at him and then disappeared. Other people have reported seeing a huge cat lurking in the shadows on the National Mall.

The catlike beast prowling Washington, DC, also comes around when there is a change in administrations.

21

ANNA SURRATT

On July 7, 1865, Mary Surratt was hanged along with three members of the group who were involved in the assassination of President Lincoln. It wasn't clear if she was part of the plot, but two very unreliable witnesses sealed her fate. Her daughter, Anna, was convinced of her innocence.

On the night before her mother's **execution**, Anna tearfully went to the White House to ask President Andrew Johnson to reverse the court's sentence of death. She forced her way to the front doors, banging loudly and crying. Security officers dragged her away. It's said that every July her ghost returns and can be heard banging on the front doors of the White House.

H STREET HAUNTING

Mary Surratt ran the boarding house on H Street where the plot to murder Lincoln was planned. Anna sold this building shortly after her mother's execution. The building frequently changed ownership as strange whispers and creaking footsteps were commonly heard. It's said the ghost of Mary Surratt will walk there restlessly until her name is cleared.

A person's spirit is said to remain after death when the spirit has unfinished business—like proving their innocence of a crime.

23

WHITE HOUSE SÉANCES

A séance (SAY-ahns) is an attempt to contact someone who is dead. Often a person who is said to be sensitive to the spirit world leads such an attempt. Over the years, people have claimed that there have been séances at the White House! Mrs. Lincoln held séances in the Green Room to try to contact her dead son, Willie. President Lincoln may have even attended, if only to comfort his grieving wife.

Some say that Eleanor Roosevelt spoke with Lincoln's ghost during a series of séances. It's rumored that Hillary Clinton contacted the ghost of Eleanor Roosevelt at a White House séance, too.

It's been said that Willie Lincoln's ghost also appeared when Ulysses S. Grant was president.

WILLIE LINCOLN

Abraham Lincoln's son Willie died at the White House when he was 11. He died of an illness called typhoid fever. His mother was so upset by this that she tried to make contact with him beyond the grave. Willie's ghost is said to haunt one of the bedrooms on the second floor.

25

A HAUNTED CITY

You can visit many other haunted places in Washington, DC! Just across from the White House, Lafayette Square is considered the most haunted place in the city. The ghost of Philip Barton Key II, son of Francis Scott Key, is said to remain near where he was shot. The ghost of naval hero Stephen Decatur is often seen at a window overlooking the park. The sad ghost of a writer's wife, Marian "Clover" Adams, returns each December to the Hay-Adams Hotel.

Ghostly figures wander the hallways of the Eisenhower Office Building nearby. Spirits are restless in the Willard Hotel, the Octagon House, and many other buildings, too.

OLD POST CHAPEL

The Old Post Chapel near Arlington National **Cemetery** has hosted thousands of funerals. Not surprisingly, it has a long history of hauntings. Doors lock and unlock. The organ plays when no one is there. Lights flicker on and off. Sometimes a Spanish woman dressed in black is seen crying softly in the chapel.

If you go to Washington, DC, keep your eyes open and your camera ready.

MORE SPOOKY STUFF

So many other eerie happenings have been reported at the White House! Here are just some of the spooky stories:

- Mary Todd Lincoln claimed that she heard Thomas Jefferson's ghost playing the violin.
- Harry Truman said of the White House: "The place is haunted, sure as shootin'!"
- Jacqueline Kennedy told a reporter that she found comfort knowing Lincoln's ghost was present at the White House.
- When Lyndon Johnson was president, his daughter Lynda said she sensed the spirit of Willie Lincoln in her room.
- Hillary Clinton has described the spooky atmosphere of the White House, especially at night.
- Congresswoman Christine Sullivan observed Lincoln's ghost by a window in 1995.
- Jenna Bush reportedly heard mysterious opera music coming from the fireplace in her bedroom.

While most White House spirits don't seem to mean any harm, their presence could scare anyone at night!

SOUNDS AND SPIRITS TO THIS DAY

First Lady Michelle Obama has told of spooky happenings at the White House. She and President Obama have been awakened by strange sounds in the hallway. Some members of their family have also reported the strange sensations of something gnawing on their feet as they were trying to sleep. It seems that mysterious spirits are still lurking about the White House today!

GLOSSARY

American Civil War: a war fought from 1861 to 1865 in the United States between the Union (the Northern states) and the Confederacy (the Southern states)

assassin: someone who kills with a sudden attack

cemetery: a place where the dead are buried

execution: the killing of someone, often for doing wrong

inaugural: having to do with the inauguration, or the event at which the president officially takes office

laundry: clothes or linens that have been cleaned or need to be cleaned

mansion: a big house

obstinate: sticking to one opinion or purpose

retaliation: to cause harm in return for a wrong

survive: to live through something

terrorist: one who uses violence and fear to challenge an authority

War of 1812: a war between the United States and Great Britain that took place from 1812 to 1815

World War II: a war fought from 1939 to 1945 that involved countries around the world

FOR MORE INFORMATION

BOOKS

Axelrod-Contrada, Joan. *The World's Most Famous Ghosts.* Mankato, MN: Capstone Press, 2012.

Belanger, Jeff. *Who's Haunting the White House?: The President's Mansion and the Ghosts Who Live There.* New York, NY: Sterling Publishing, 2008.

Kenney, Karen Latchana. *The White House.* Edina, MN: Magic Wagon, 2011.

WEBSITES

About the White House

www.whitehouse.gov/about

Learn more about the president's house, and take an interactive tour to see the haunted spots in this book.

Ghosts in the White House

www.history.com/topics/ghosts-in-the-white-house

Read and watch videos about the ghosts that haunt the White House.

INDEX